TAPE

BY STEPHEN BELBER

DRAMATISTS
PLAY SERVICE
INC.

SPECIAL NOTE

Anyone receiving permission to produce TAPE is required to give credit to the Author as sole and exclusive Author of the Play on the title page of all programs distributed in connection with performances of the Play and in all instances in which the title of the Play appears for purposes of advertising, publicizing or otherwise exploiting the Play and/or a production thereof. The name of the Author must appear on a separate line, in which no other name appears, immediately beneath the title and in size of type equal to 50% of the size of the largest, most prominent letter used for the title of the Play. No person, firm or entity may receive credit larger or more prominent than that accorded the Author. The following acknowledgments must appear on the title page in all programs distributed in connection with performances of the Play:

Originally developed and workshopped at the Access Theater, New York City,
Jacqueline Christy, Artistic Director.

Premiered in the 2000 Humana Festival of New American Plays
at Actors Theatre of Louisville,
Jon Jory, Artistic Director, opening February 29, 2000.

Tape was subsequently produced by Naked Angels
in New York City on January 17, 2002,
Tim Ransom, Artistic Director; Ilana Levine and Sherri Kotimsky, Producers.

Special thanks and gratitude to
Jeremy Norton, Josh Stamberg and Dominic Fumusa.

TAPE was originally developed and workshopped at the Access Theater (Jacqueline Christy, Artistic Director) in New York City on May 6, 1999. It was directed by Steven Pickering; the set design was by Charles Kirby; the lighting design was by Tyler Micoleau; and the stage manager was Susanna Harris. The cast was as follows:

VINCE .... Dominic Fumusa
JON .... Josh Stamberg
AMY .... Phoebe Jonas

TAPE premiered in the 2000 Humana Festival of New American Plays at Actors Theatre of Louisville (Jon Jory, Artistic Director) in Louisville, Kentucky, on February 29, 2000. It was directed by Brian Jucha; the set design was by Paul Owen; the lighting design was by Greg Sullivan; the sound design was by Martin Desjardins; the costume design was by Suttirat Larlarb; the stage manager was Charles M. Turner III; and the dramaturg was Michael Bigelow Dixon. The cast was as follows:

VINCE .... Dominic Fumusa
JON .... Stephen Kunken
AMY .... Erica Yoder

TAPE premiered in New York City at the Jose Quintero Theater on January 17, 2002. It was presented by Naked Angels Theater Company (Ilana Levine and Sherri Kotimsky, Producers; Tim Ransom, Artistic Director). It was directed by Geoffrey Nauffts; the set design was by George Xenos; the lighting design was by Greg Macpherson; the sound design was by Roger Raines; the costume design was by Sarah Beers; and the stage manager was Peggy Samuels. The cast was as follows:

VINCE .... Dominic Fumusa
JON .... Josh Stamberg
AMY .... Alison West

CHARACTERS

VINCE: beat-up jeans, no shoes, maybe a tank top T-shirt; lovable, self-destructive type.

JON: dressed casually but well, with a degree of "hip" thrown in — V-neck sweater, no T-shirt; retro, perfectly fitting jeans, worn leather jacket, brown leather shoes.

AMY: dressed casually — the way a young attorney might be on a Friday night.

PLACE

A Motel 6 motel room, Lansing, Michigan.

TIME

The present.

TAPE

A Motel 6 motel room, Lansing, Michigan. Music — perhaps Eddie Cochrane — plays loudly. Vince, twenty-eight, stands alone at the sink outside the bathroom pouring the contents of a can of Schlitz into the sink with one hand while holding and drinking from a second can of Schlitz in the other. When the first can is empty, he chucks it casually onto the floor. He opens another can from a six-pack which rests on the sink and repeats the action. When it is empty, he tosses it across the room. At about this time, he finishes the beer he is drinking and throws it towards the TV. He opens another beer to drink and another one to empty. But first, he takes off his blue jeans and throws them on the bed. He returns to his task of emptying beers. Eventually, there is a knock on the door. Vince finishes emptying the beer and chucks it onto one of the beds as he goes to answer. He takes a moment to muss his hair, then opens ... Jon, twenty-eight, enters. They hug. Several seconds.

VINCE. Hey, man!
JON. Hey, Vince! *(They hug — warm, genuine, an obviously old friendship.)*
VINCE. Welcome to my palazzio!
JON. This is great, man!
VINCE. Yeah! —
JON. This is great! —
VINCE. How are you?
JON. Can't complain.
VINCE. Cool!
JON. Totally. It is, I'm very psyched.
VINCE. You should be, Jonny, it's a great thing.
JON. Thanks, man. Thanks. *(They hug again.)*

VINCE. And you know what else? — It's great to be alive!

JON. Totally! *(Beat.)* What's up?

VINCE. Not much.

JON. You're not dressed.

VINCE. Lay off.

JON. It's not that I don't like it —

VINCE. But — ?

JON. But nothing.

VINCE. So — ?

JON. So nothing —

VINCE. OK!

JON. OK.

VINCE. Excellent!

JON. Fine. *(Beat; a smile.)* I swear to God you get stranger each year.

VINCE. You look good, Jon. *(Jon enters the room more fully now, looking around.)*

JON. Where's Leah?

VINCE. Didn't make the trip.

JON. Why not?

VINCE. We broke up.

JON. Shut up.

VINCE. I'm serious —

JON. Shut up —

VINCE. I'm serious —

JON. You broke up?!

VINCE. We broke up.

JON. Why? —

VINCE. Complicated —

JON. Why? —

VINCE. She didn't like the way I dress.

JON. Don't joke —

VINCE. I'm not.

JON. What happened?

VINCE. I get stranger each year.

JON. 'Vince —

VINCE. She thinks I'm a dick. *(Pause.)* She sends apologies for not coming. She says she's sure it'll go well.

JON. *(Pause.)* I don't believe it.

VINCE. I'm serious, man, she does —

JON. Why did you break up?

VINCE. I don't know. *(Silence.)*

JON. I'm sorry, man.

VINCE. Me too.

JON. *(Beat.)* Is it permanent?

VINCE. Permanent as a dead horse, amigo.

JON. *(Beat.)* Did you do something?

VINCE. Why do you say that?

JON. Because I know you.

VINCE. *You* think I'm a dick —

JON. No, it's just that I know that you occasionally have a tendency to *act* in a phallic fashion.

VINCE. I'm not like that anymore.

JON. What — you're not a dick?

VINCE. See what I mean?

JON. I'm just asking what happened.

VINCE. Lots of things.

JON. Like? —

VINCE. Like she thinks I'm reckless.

JON. In general?

VINCE. Yes.

JON. *(Pause.)* Were you at all *specifically* reckless recently?

VINCE. Not particularly specifically.

JON. Be honest —

VINCE. I am.

JON. Did you fuck around?

VINCE. No!

JON. Vince? —

VINCE. I didn't!

JON. So what happened?

Vince. She says I have violent tendencies.

JON. ... Oh boy ...

VINCE. I never touched her, Jon.

JON. I didn't say you did.

VINCE. It's just that she *thinks* I have "unresolved issues which occasionally manifest themselves in potentially violent ways."

(Beat.) What?

JON. I think it's fair to say she has a point.

VINCE. No one's saying she doesn't have a point.

JON. So — ?

VINCE. So she has to break up with me?

JON. She's probably scared.

VINCE. Of what? I never threatened her.

JON. You present a threatening appearance.

VINCE. Dude, we've been together *three* years!

JON. So?

VINCE. So you think she'd be used to it by now!

JON. It's a tricky one, Vin.

VINCE. What're you talking about?

JON. I'm just saying, it's tricky. Women these days have no reason to hang around potentially violent guys. It's not an attractive quality to them anymore. Too many other guys out there with *resolved* violent tendencies.

VINCE. So I'm just out of fashion?

JON. Don't be a fool —

VINCE. Don't be a politically correct fuck! —

JON. I'm not, I'm telling you that you're an idiot if you think chicks are gonna put up with your bullshit.

VINCE. What bullshit? —

JON. Like playing rough —

VINCE. I didn't play rough with her.

JON. Vince —

VINCE. What? —

JON. I love you —

VINCE. Good —

JON. — but c'mon.

VINCE. What? —

JON. You don't *not* play rough.

VINCE. I totally *do* not play rough.

JON. You're swarthy.

VINCE. That's a stereotype.

JON. True.

VINCE. Bigot.

JON. I can't be a bigot — I'm a Jew.

10

VINCE. I know plenty of Jewish bigots.

JON. Who?

VINCE. Irving Berlin.

JON. *(Beat.)* OK, let's move on to the next subject —

VINCE. Fine.

JON. I'm sorry you guys broke up. Really. I'm sorry for you both.

VINCE. *(Aside.)* Don't be sorry for *that* bitch ...

JON. Fine, I'm just sorry for you. Next subject. *(Beat.)*

VINCE. She says if I get my act together, stick with the meetings and stop being a dick, she might consider talking to me again. *(Jon gives a slight kick to one of the empty beer cans on the floor.)*

JON. Good. *(Beat.)* Should we get some dinner?

VINCE. I gotta wait for a call.

JON. From who?

VINCE. None of your business.

JON. Leah?

VINCE. *(Indignant.)* No.

JON. ... O-K. *(Silence.)*

VINCE. *(Sulky.)* So are you ready for tomorrow?

JON. You're mad.

VINCE. I'm not mad —

JON. You're allowed to be —

VINCE. I'm not mad. I'll find someone else.

JON. It's true —

VINCE. Who *appreciates* my dark side.

JON. Exactly. *(Pause.)* But the thing is, if you could maybe find a way to learn something from this, then you won't have as *large* of a dark side.

VINCE. *(Beat.)* Learn what?

JON. Learn to deal with some of your violent desires.

VINCE. *(Skeptical.)* How?

JON. By acknowledging them, by making some type of truce with yourself where you're not always in constant battle to prove your integrity, or your self-worth or whatever it is that you think nobody gets about you.

VINCE. I don't think there's anything to get about me. I'm a simple man.

JON. Yeah, but your idea of manhood is putting on Eddie

Cochrane and screwing your girl. It's not like that anymore. Women want other things.

VINCE. Like what?

JON. I don't know. *(Beat.)* ... Enya.

VINCE. *(Beat; unconvinced.)* Yeah. *(Silence.)*

JON. Vince —

VINCE. So where're you staying?

JON. *(Pause.)* They got me over at the Radisson in town.

VINCE. *NICE!!*

JON. Yeah, it is.

VINCE. Lansing Film Festival!

JON. Yeah, that and Cannes.

VINCE. Still, it's a good gig.

JON. It's a good cheap thrill.

VINCE. Why do you have to dump on it? — It's a good gig.

JON. Because I have big expectations. I spent two years on this film, I want it to be in a theater near you.

VINCE. *(Re: window.)* It is.

JON. Yeah, but you had to come out to the middle of fucking Michigan to be there. For *one* screening, for which I'm getting paid a whopping five hundred bucks.

VINCE. Yeah, but all you need is for one guy from — whatever — from Disney to be there tomorrow — he likes it — boom, next thing you know, you're directing *Free Willy Four.*

JON. Starring David Hasselhoff.

VINCE. Hey —

JON. Hey —

VINCE. Hey —

JON. Hey. *(Beat.)* Dude, I'm starving.

VINCE. What time is it?

JON. *(Re: watch.)* Quarter of.

VINCE. You wanna a beer?

JON. Aren't you supposed to be getting your act together?

VINCE. I'll do it when I get back.

JON. See, this is what she's talking about —

VINCE. Jon — if I wanted to hang out with my mother ... right?

JON. Well put.

VINCE. What Leah doesn't know won't hurt her. *(Vince carefully*

12

and rather deliberately reaches into his bag. Beat.)

JON. Whattayou got goin' on in that bag, Vince?

VINCE. Beer.

JON. How much?

VINCE. Lot. *(Vince tosses Jon a beer, then opens one for himself.)*

JON. I don't know why I said you had violent tendencies.

VINCE. Why? —

JON. Warm beer, boxers, Motel 6. Who needs Betty Ford?

VINCE. We can't *all* be at the Radisson.

JON. Hey — you know, if you wanna stay with me —

VINCE. No.

JON. Seriously, I thought you'd be with Leah, that's why I didn't offer earlier —

VINCE. It's not a problem —

JON. It's *not* a problem — they gave me a double; eleventh floor overlooking a park —

VINCE. No, man, you probably wanna get laid.

JON. *(Pause.)* That's true.

VINCE. It's your big weekend, chicks are gonna flock to you.

JON. You're right.

VINCE. I'll be fine here.

JON. Cool.

VINCE. Should I twist your arm?

JON. Yeah. More.

VINCE. Schmuck —

JON. Prick —

VINCE. Putz —

JON. Suck-ass. *(Beat.)* I appreciate you coming out here. Seriously. We've come a long way.

VINCE. Since — ?

JON. I dunno. High school.

VINCE. You think?

JON. Some of us. *(Pause.)* Dude, I'm totally giving you shit.

VINCE. No but you're right —

JON. No I'm not —

VINCE. You are, face it —

JON. I'm right only in that I think you can do better than you are.

VINCE. Why? —

13

JON. Because I believe in you. If I didn't, we wouldn't still be friends *and* I wouldn't be able to say that to you.

VINCE. Why not?

JON. Because it sounds totally pretentious.

VINCE. You're right —

JON. But the thing is — I mean it. I'm sorry but it's true. It's like this thing with Leah — if it *is* permanent, then you should view it as an opportunity to change —

VINCE. Change *what?*

JON. I don't know — find a new job, new way of doing things —

VINCE. I like my job.

JON. What *is* your job?

VINCE. Volunteer firefighter.

JON. I know, but how do you make your money?

VINCE. Lay off.

JON. I'm just saying —

VINCE. What?

JON. — it's immature.

VINCE. *You* try doing it —

JON. That's not the point —

VINCE. Besides, the majority of my clients happen to be over fifty. If that's not mature, I'm baffled as to what is.

JON. Private dope delivery to ex-hippies does not a mature man make, Vince. It's not that different than standing on the corner selling to teenagers —

VINCE. Why're you lecturing me?

JON. I'm not, I'm just pointing things out —

VINCE. Such as? —

JON. Such as I think you can do better.

VINCE. Than what? —

JON. Than pissing your life away. You're a smart guy, why're you still dealing drugs?

VINCE. *Because* I'm smart. If I was dumb, I would've gotten caught by now. Besides — I'm a firefighter.

JON. You *deal* to the fire *chief,* Vince!

VINCE. He *needs* me!

JON. That's not the point —

VINCE. Why is what you do better?!

JON. Why is what I do better?

VINCE. Yeah.

JON. *(Pause.)* What I'm *trying* to do is better because it's an attempt at figuring things out. I would like to, eventually, become good enough at it to the point where I can contribute to a larger debate about why this country is so fucked up. I would like to try and examine why it is that a fifty-whatever-year-old fire chief feels the need to get stoned every night. What is it about life in America that's driving that urge in him?

VINCE. He *likes* it?

JON. Fine, but then there's something slightly wrong with the fact that someone with that type of responsibility is constantly *high.* There's maybe some sort of symbolism there worth examining.

VINCE. His firehouse happens to have the best record in the city —

JON. Vince — if my house was on fire, I wouldn't want his high ass anywhere *near* it —

VINCE. You're such a fucking bigot! —

JON. The guy has a good record because he's *lucky!* —

VINCE. Says who?

JON. It's obvious! He's living a big, luck-driven lie!

VINCE. What're you — high?

JON. I'm serious —

VINCE. You're making movies about people who rob *Popeye's Fried Chicken!* —

JON. I'm telling a story which aims to resonate the notion of where our society's headed if we're not careful. The only reason it sounds pompous is because I haven't fully honed my skills yet.

VINCE. It doesn't sound pompous, it sounds like you're talking out your ass —

JON. Why?

VINCE. Because you have no idea where society is headed. You're just like everybody else — you're following the latest trend which you hope will get you laid until the trend switches to something else, at which point you'll drop the old one and make a movie about — whatever — like turtles that get caught in fishing nets. Starring ... *Cindy* Hasselhoff. *(Beat.)* His niece.

JON. *(Wounded ...)* You don't like my work?

VINCE. I like it like I like a shot of whiskey first thing in the morning — it's good for about ten minutes, then I want my coffee.

JON. *(Beat.)* Wow.

VINCE. What?

JON. Did I say something to piss you off? Or is it that you're just a dick?

VINCE. Both.

JON. Good to see that you're finally admitting it.

VINCE. Unlike some of us.

JON. What — that *I'm* a dick?

VINCE. Ah — yeah.

JON. When?

VINCE. I'm speaking figuratively.

JON. When was I figuratively a dick?

VINCE. High school.

JON. I was too shy to be a dick in high school.

VINCE. Oh I think you held your own.

JON. That's because *everyone's* a dick in high school, Vince. It's the white-male-football-playing prerogative. The trick is to evolve into something else once you're out.

VINCE. Jon, you're wearing two-hundred-dollar shoes.

JON. First of all, that's not true —

VINCE. One-fifty.

JON. I'm less shy than in high school.

VINCE. So you're an *overt* dick?

JON. No, actually, I'm a thoughtful person who wears nice shoes —

VINCE. And is occasionally full of shit.

JON. Is there something I'm not doing that you want me to do, Vince?

VINCE. I don't want you to do anything.

JON. No? — because it seems like I'm being asked to do something by a twenty-eight-year-old pot dealer who refuses to progress with the rest of the world — which would be OK if it were a legitimate *rebellion* instead of just some lonely guy hanging out in his boxer shorts acting like a potentially violent dick!

VINCE. *(Beat.)* You wanna get high?

JON. No.

VINCE. C'mon, Jon, get high —

16

JON. I'm not getting high —

VINCE. Why — only violent dicks get high? —

JON. No —

VINCE. So let's get high —

JON. I'm *not* getting high —

VINCE. *I* am! *(Vince goes into his duffel bag and carefully and deliberately searches around.)*

JON. Whattayou got goin' on in that bag, Vince?

VINCE. Pot.

JON. How much?

VINCE. Lot. *(He produces a very well-rolled joint, lights up and takes a large hit, then offers it to Jon, who refuses ... but then, after extreme and exaggerated efforts by Vince, relents and accepts. They smoke in silence ...)* You know who's out here?

JON. Where?

VINCE. Here. Lansing.

JON. Who?

VINCE. Amy Randall.

JON. *(Pause.)* Really?

VINCE. Yep. I heard that from Tracy about two years ago, then when you got this thing, I looked her up on the Net, and she's out here. She's like ... an assistant county prosecutor or something.

JON. Did you call her?

VINCE. *(Pause.)* I thought about it.

JON. You should, especially now that Leah's ...

VINCE. Out of the picture?

JON. Yeah.

VINCE. Yeah.

JON. *(Pause.)* I wonder if she's still ...

VINCE. Hot?

JON. Yeah.

VINCE. That's not a very politically appropriate way to think about women, Jon.

JON. OK — here's the thing with being appropriate: It's better to try and do that than to be a *complete* asshole. The choice to respect people is actually a *good* one, despite people like you who insist on calling fat people "fat" to their face.

VINCE. What if they're fat?

17

JON. If they're fat they probably already *realize* it without your having to remind them. It basically has to do with having a couple *manners.*

VINCE. Is that what it is?

JON. That's it.

VINCE. So why'd you ask if she was hot?

JON. Because she is. Was. It's not a bad word. If the word is essentially a compliment, then saying it isn't bad manners. Human beings like to be called attractive. I'm not labeling Amy Randall anything she doesn't already know. And I'm sure she's smart, too.

VINCE. Well if we call her and she weighs three hundred and twenty pounds, then I think we should go up to her and say, "Gee, we're really glad we dated you in high school instead of now because in high school you were really hot and now ... well, I'm sure you already *realize* about now."

JON. You know what, Vince? — why don't you shut up for awhile.

VINCE. Oh I see — I made a point so now I have to shut up?

JON. No, it's that you like being rude for the sake of it; either that or you do it to prove that nobody can *make* you be nice. Either way, it gets tiresome. And the thing is, you and I don't see each other often enough to make worthwhile this little competition for "who's more authentic." It's not about that anymore. OK? We should just accept the fact that we're a little different from each other, and let the friendship go from there.

VINCE. "Accept the fact that we're a little different from each other"?

JON. Yeah.

VINCE. *(Pause ...)* Would you like to make me?

JON. Make you what?

VINCE. Make me "accept that fact."

JON. No.

VINCE. Why not?

JON. 'Cause it's stupid.

VINCE. No it's not —

JON. Yes it is —

VINCE. No it's not because how else will I know that you're different?

18

JON. You'll just have to trust me.

VINCE. No. Prove it.

JON. Or else what?

VINCE. *(Matter of fact.)* I kick your ass.

JON. *(Pause.)* I guess this means you're potentially violent.

VINCE. *(Quiet menace.)* Only when it comes to you, Jon.

JON. *(Beat.)* Funny how you get this way every time we talk about Amy Randall.

VINCE. No I don't.

JON. I don't even think you realize it, Vince.

VINCE. Fuck off.

JON. OK, you know what? — I'm outta here —

VINCE. Fuck off —

JON. Thanks for coming —

VINCE. Fuck off —

JON. Vincent.

VINCE. Fuck *you,* Jon! —

JON. Look — I'm sorry you still feel bad about Amy Randall, and that every time you get stoned and drunk around me this comes up. But it was ten years ago; I've explained to you a million times that I felt that it was OK for me to be with her because you guys had broken up, and that I now have a better understanding as to the *fragility* of human emotions — especially those belonging to swarthy Italian-Americans like yourself — and thus if the situation arose again today, I wouldn't let what happened happen. But these things *do* happen, especially in high school, and I'm sorry I hurt your feelings.

VINCE. *(Pause.)* That's not what I'm talking about.

JON. What're you talking about?

VINCE. I'm talking about what happened.

JON. So am I.

VINCE. So what happened?

JON. We slept together.

VINCE. How?

JON. What do you mean?

VINCE. How did you sleep together?

JON. OK — so now this is about that?

VINCE. Isn't it?

JON. Is it?

VINCE. *You* tell *me.*

JON. We slept together.

VINCE. How?

JON. You *know* how.

VINCE. No, actually, I don't. I have an idea, but I don't *know* because we've never actually *talked* about it. We've *laughed* about it; we thought it was kinda *funny,* but you've never exactly *told* me what happened.

JON. So what do you wanna know?

VINCE. I wanna know what happened.

JON. We slept together.

VINCE. How?

JON. What do you mean "how"?

VINCE. *How!*

JON. You have to be more specific, Vince.

VINCE. In what fashion did you sleep with her?

JON. We had sex.

VINCE. And — ?

JON. And that was it.

VINCE. Was it good sex?

JON. I've had better since.

VINCE. Was it fun?

JON. It was all right.

VINCE. Was it on the rough side?

JON. Hard to say. We were both drunk.

VINCE. Did you rape her?

JON. *(Beat ... Thinks he's joking.)* No.

VINCE. Kind of?

JON. No!

VINCE. Was it like date rape?

JON. "*Like* date rape"?

VINCE. Did you "kind of" force her to have sex with you?

JON. No!! *(Silence.)*

VINCE. Jon?

JON. I'm not sure what you want me to say, Vince.

VINCE. I want you to tell me what happened. *You're* a filmmaker — lay out the scene for me; show me the dailies.

JON. Can we talk about this sometime when you're not high?

VINCE. Maybe the only reason I'm high is so that *you* get high so that for once you can tell me the truth instead of changing the subject.

JON. *(Beat.)* Yes, it was a little rough. Which is obviously something that doesn't make me proud.

VINCE. *(Beat.)* Did you ever talk to her after that?

JON. No.

VINCE. Why not?

JON. Because I wouldn't know what to say to her. I'm a completely different person than I was then.

VINCE. Maybe she is too.

JON. May-be.

VINCE. Maybe she's fat.

JON. That's really not funny.

VINCE. I didn't say it was. *(Beat.)* Does anyone else know what happened?

JON. *I* didn't tell anyone.

VINCE. Maybe you should.

JON. I don't actually consider it a crime, Vince. It was not a good thing; it was morally somewhat questionable and I wish it hadn't happened, but I don't think it's the type of thing where I need to turn myself into the police ten years later.

VINCE. I'm not talking about the police.

JON. So what're you talking about?

VINCE. I dunno. Her.

JON. I think she already knows.

VINCE. Maybe you should apologize.

JON. Oh Jesus —

VINCE. What?

JON. You want me to *apologize* to her?

VINCE. Why not?

JON. It wasn't even date rape, Vince! — It was just something that got a little out of hand —

VINCE. I thought you weren't sure what date rape was.

JON. Look — I'm sorry.

VINCE. Don't apologize to me.

JON. *(Recomposing.)* I'm not. What I'm trying to say is that ten

21

years ago I did something wrong, and when I think about it now, it seems like the person who did that is a complete stranger to me. A dumb, drunk, high-school senior who thought she was just being a little prudish and needed some coercion. It was bad and I regret it but it was a far cry from rape. And I don't think *she* would look back on it and call it that either.

VINCE. What *would* she call it? —

JON. I don't know what she'd call it —

VINCE. What if she called it rape? —

JON. Listen to me, I highly, highly doubt that she even remembers it —

VINCE. *You* remember it —

JON. I remember it because it was a pivotal thing for me —

VINCE. Your *first* rape?

JON. Stop being an asshole —

VINCE. Tell me why it was pivotal.

JON. Because it was one of the first times I looked at myself objectively and decided that I would try to avoid becoming a certain type of person. OK? For her it might have been nothing particularly important one way or another; for me, it constituted something more significant.

VINCE. So you'd like to think.

JON. Why are you suddenly high and mighty? —

VINCE. I'm not high and mighty — I'm too *high* to be high and mighty! I'm just a lowly, drug-dealing, boxer-wearing scum of the earth.

JON. You said it —

VINCE. No, actually, *you* did —

JON. I didn't mean it like that —

VINCE. How'd you mean it? —

JON. That you should change your life a bit —

VINCE. This coming from a rapist —

JON. You're an idiot —

VINCE. Sorry — this coming from a big low-budget moviemaker who makes movies about "where society is possibly headed if we can just manage to forget about that date rape we didn't *kind of* really commit in high school."

JON. You're seriously disturbed.

VINCE. No, actually, I *am* high and mighty. I was wrong before.

JON. What do you want me to say, Vince? — I'm sorry.

VINCE. Stop apologizing to *me*, Jon —

JON. I'm not! I'm apologizing in general. I wish it had never happened. I don't think I'm an evil person.

VINCE. No one's saying you're evil —

JON. It sure as hell feels like it —

VINCE. Do *you* think you're evil?

JON. No —

VINCE. So then you're not evil. *I'm* the evil one here. You're the morally conscious movie-maker.

JON. Whatever —

VINCE. Whatever —

JON. Can we stop now? —

VINCE. Totally —

JON. Thank you —

VINCE. *(Beats ...)* I just think you should call her.

JON. I'm not gonna call her.

VINCE. I think you should —

JON. Stop! OK? To call her would be to trivialize the entire matter. It would be like saying, "How's life — oh by the way, sorry I date-raped you ten years ago."

VINCE. So you *did* date-rape her?

JON. No, I didn't —

VINCE. What *did* you do?

JON. I coerced her to have sex with me.

VINCE. How?

JON. Verbally.

VINCE. You verbally coerced her?

JON. Yes. *(Pause ...)* By applying excessive linguistic pressure, I persuaded her to have sex with me.

VINCE. And *then* things got rough?

JON. Things got rough in that after awhile they became aggressively playful.

VINCE. *They* did?

JON. We did.

VINCE. Meaning what?

JON. Meaning I probably still thought I was being playful but

23

others might interpret my actions as being rough.

VINCE. — i.e., rape.

JON. No — rough.

VINCE. Look — Jon, only you two know what happened, so only you two can "interpret" your actions. So why don't you just tell me the facts and interpret them later.

JON. I'm telling you — I argued her into it —

VINCE. You're fucking *lying,* Jon! *(Silence.)*

JON. What is your problem?

VINCE. How can you sit here with your oldest friend in the world and continuously tell lies?

JON. What makes you think I'm lying?

VINCE. Because only *you* would come up with the term "excessive linguistic pressure." That's not a normal expression, Jon, it's a clear sign of excessive bullshit. If you had really done only that, you'd be more specific. You'd say that you told her that if she didn't put out you'd start telling people she had V.D., or smelled bad, or had a penis, or any of the *normal* things that guys say. But *you* come up with your typical crap, which *sounds* mature but contains *nothing!* But it's bullshit, because the reason you are where you are today is because you always insist on getting things your way. It's what you're good at, Jon, so why don't you just own up and admit what you did?!

JON. *(Beat.)* Fuck off, Vince. *(Jon heads for the door.)*

VINCE. Fine. *I'll* call her. *(Vince reaches for the phone.)*

JON. Don't do that.

VINCE. Why not? —

JON. Because I would like you not to —

VINCE. Why not? —

JON. Because you've already made your point —

VINCE. What's my point? —

JON. Your point is that nobody's perfect, including me, so it offends you when I tell you how I think you should live your life.

VINCE. That's not my point —

JON. It should be —

VINCE. It's not —

JON. Why? —

VINCE. Because I haven't gotten to my point yet —

JON. So then get to it —

VINCE. Maybe I don't have one —

JON. Then I'm gonna go —

VINCE. Wrong —

JON. No — right. *(Jon starts for the door but Vince beats him to it. Vince locks the door and stands firmly in front of it.)*

VINCE. Admit it.

JON. Admit what?

VINCE. What you did to Amy.

JON. What even makes you think I did something?

VINCE. Because I know —

JON. How? —

VINCE. Because she told me —

JON. Told you what? —

VINCE. What you did —

JON. What did she say? —

VINCE. What? —

JON. What did she say?

VINCE. ... Nothing.

JON. Get outta my way, Vincent.

VINCE. It was obvious — *(Jon reaches for the door handle only to have Vince shove him forcefully in the chest. The confrontation has reached a whole new level.)* Tell me what you did and I'll let you go.

JON. Stop being a dick —

VINCE. Tell me what you did —

JON. Why do you care?

VINCE. 'Cause I wanna hear it —

JON. What would that change?

VINCE. I don't know! —

JON. So then what does it matter? — we both know I did something wrong! —

VINCE. So then tell me! —

JON. I pinned her arms back and stuck my dick in! OK?! For Christ fucking sakes! Shit happens! I already said I'm sorry! *(Silence ...)*

VINCE. Thank you. *(Vince steps away from Jon, goes to his duffel bag, reaches inside and carefully rummages around for a second. Jon looks on with exhaustion and curiosity. After a moment, Vince takes out a small tape recorder from the bag. He looks at it briefly to make sure it is still running, then presses the "stop" button. He then places the tape*

25

recorder on the floor in front of him. Beat. Jon, having registered the import of this, stares at the recorder, and then at Vince. More silence.)

JON. What the hell did you just do?

VINCE. Taped our conversation.

JON. *(Pause.)* Why?

VINCE. I wanted to make sure I heard you right. *(Beat; Vince picks up the recorder, presses "rewind" briefly, then presses "play." Tape: "I pinned her arms back and stuck my dick in! OK?! For Christ fucking sakes! Shit happens!" Vince presses "stop." Beat.)* I guess you're right — you *are* a completely different person.

JON. *(Hollow shock.)* I can't believe you just did that. *(Vince now takes a sticker label for the tape and writes on it, then methodically places the label onto the tape. He then puts the tape in the pocket of his pants, which lay strewn on the bed. He puts his pants on. He then goes to his bag once more and takes out two beers.)*

VINCE. Beer? *(Jon does not respond, still staring in disbelief at the recorder. Vince tosses the beer anyway. Without looking up, Jon "swacks" the beer out of midair, back in the direction of Vince. Beat. Vince picks up the fallen beer from the floor.)* You're mad?

JON. How could you do something like that?

VINCE. Like what?

JON. I'm not messing around, Vince —

VINCE. It offends you?

JON. It offends me fucking immensely.

VINCE. Why?

JON. I'm not even ...

VINCE. All I'm suggesting is that you call her up and apologize for the actions of a drunk high-school senior.

JON. *(Pause.)* You know you just ended our friendship.

VINCE. It's a cheap little tape recorder. It's Kmart, man.

JON. Why did you do that?

VINCE. I'm trying to make a point.

JON. Which is what?

VINCE. That there's something wrong here.

JON. Where? — With you and me?

VINCE. *(Firm.)* Yeah. And everyone else.

JON. You think that everyone else in the world should call up and apologize for what they've done wrong in their life?

VINCE. I don't know.

JON. You honestly think that would *help?* You don't think it'd just end up being a bunch of hypocrites walking around raping people and apologizing?

VINCE. You have a better idea?

JON. *(Firm.)* Yeah — not do it next time.

VINCE. That's it?

JON. Yeah.

VINCE. You don't even think she'd want it for herself?

JON. Want *what?*

VINCE. The tape.

JON. Why would she want it?

VINCE. To know that you admitted it.

JON. I doubt she even remembers it happening, Vince.

VINCE. So then she might wanna be reminded.

JON. Why?

VINCE. Because *I'd* wanna be reminded if you pinned down my arms and fucked *me* without permission.

JON. Don't talk like that —

VINCE. That's what you did, Jon, it's on the tape.

JON. This is ridiculous!

VINCE. Why?

JON. Because my apologizing now won't make a difference to her. She's probably dealt with the whole issue and moved on.

VINCE. Maybe she has, but if you're such a different guy than you were ten years ago, then you technically shouldn't have a problem apologizing for something that, in effect, the *real* you didn't even do. Now, on the other hand, if you're still the kind of guy who *could* do something like that, then I can understand your feeling hesitant to apologize. Wouldn't want to come across as a hypocrite.

JON. *(Beat.)* Give me the tape.

VINCE. No way.

JON. Why not?

VINCE. Because as you imply to me on a daily basis whenever we spend the day together — I wouldn't have the guts to *tell* her all the interesting tidbits that this tape herewith contains. It'll be much easier to simply *hand* it to her. If I even have the guts to do *that. (Vince goes into his duffel bag again and takes out a tiny plastic bag. He goes to the table and lays out three lines of coke, arranging them carefully with the edge of a credit card taken from his pocket.)* I think I'm gonna skip dinner. I'm not really hungry. *(He snorts a line of coke.)*

JON. You're not gonna give her that tape, Vince.

VINCE. Hard to say.

JON. Tell me what you're gonna do with it.

VINCE. Hard to say. *(He snorts another line of coke.)*

JON. Stop being a dick.

VINCE. I'm sorry — did you want some?

JON. What are you gonna do with the tape?

VINCE. Well ... I was *thinking about* making it into a movie and applying to next year's Lansing Film Festival. *(Sits at table calmly.)* Seriously, you should go. *(Beat.)* I'll tell her you said hello.

JON. What're you talking about?

VINCE. She should be calling at any minute.

JON. Why?

VINCE. 'Cause she said she'd call me at eight.

JON. I thought you said you didn't call her.

VINCE. No, I said I *thought* about calling her. And I actually *did*. It's cool. We're hooking up for dinner. *(Vince sits at the table, placing the tape in front of him. He snorts the last line of coke.)* Really, Jon, you should go. I mean, I probably won't even follow through with the whole thing. *(Beat.)* Unless of course, she sees it sitting there and keeps pestering me about what it is. *(Beats. Vince sips his beer. Jon does not know whether to stay or go. Beat. The phone rings. Vince looks at Jon, faux shock ... then answers. Sweet as pie:)* Hello? ... Hey, Amy! How are you? ... Yeah? Well, are you still up for some chow? ... Cool. By the way, did I tell you why I was out here? ... That's true, the film festival, but the reason for that is because — well you remember Jon Saltzman, right? ... Yeah? Well he's actually made a movie that's being shown as *part* of the festival, so I came out for that ... huh? ... Yeah, he *is* out here, staying at the Radisson ... hmm-hmm, eleventh floor, overlooking a park. Anyway, so, I don't know how you wanna work this, I'm over at the Motel 6 on Saginaw ... exactly ... cool, well only thing is that I don't have wheels, so maybe — ... well that'd be great, if you wanna just pick me up and we can take it from there ... Great, so

28

you know where it is? … Cool, I'm in room thirty-two … OK, I'll see you in a few … Bye now. *(He hangs up the phone and begins to get dressed.)* Dude, can I borrow a couple bucks?

JON. Why are you doing this?

VINCE. Well, at first it was a moral crusade, but now I'm not really sure except for the fact that you don't want me to.

JON. And that's worth more than our entire friendship?

VINCE. Jon, if you weren't my oldest friend, I don't think I would have ever assumed that I possess the power to make you think twice about something like this. Assuming you *are* thinking twice.

JON. There are better ways to go about making someone do that.

VINCE. How? Convince you with a really good argument? Apply excessive linguistic pressure? *(No answer.)* I'm not a very moral guy, Jon, much less a highly articulate poet-moviemaker. I can barely pay my rent much less persuade someone like *you* to stop being an asshole.

JON. No one's asking you to be articulate, Vince, it's just that you pick potentially the most important weekend of my life to bring up something I haven't even *thought* about in ten years!

VINCE. *(Beat.)* Yeah. I guess so. *(Vince is now full dressed and ready to go.)* You gonna stay here?

JON. Give me the tape.

VINCE. No.

JON. Give me the tape, Vince.

VINCE. Why?

JON. Because it doesn't belong to you.

VINCE. I *bought* it at Kmart!!!

JON. What's *on* it doesn't belong —

VINCE. Bullshit! I had to be like Aldrich fucking Ames to make this tape. It's the most planned-out thing I've done my whole life!

JON. It's *mine*.

VINCE. I'm gonna give it to you and you're gonna destroy it.

JON. No I'm not.

VINCE. What're you gonna do? — Put it in your closet and not think about it for *another* ten years?

JON. Where did you get this whole self-righteous thing? It's really not like you to have a spine.

VINCE. What can I say? I'm a fireman.

29

JON. *(Sitting on bed.)* I'm not leaving until you give it up.

VINCE. I don't care if you're not leaving, just don't finish my coke.

JON. Tell me something — have you ever done something that you regretted?

VINCE. Yes —

JON. That you never apologized for? —

VINCE. Yes —

JON. So then why're you doing this now?

VINCE. I don't know! It must be because I have guilt about all that stuff I never apologized for and I'm taking it out on you!

JON. OK, so then it's irrational.

VINCE. I agree —

JON. So give me the tape —

VINCE. No fucking way! *(Beat.)* You know, I wasn't even gonna give it to her at all, but the way you're acting, it's like I have no choice. *(Silence.)* She was on her cell, man. Said she was five minutes away.

JON. Give me the tape.

VINCE. No.

JON. Vincent —

VINCE. What?

JON. Give me the tape —

VINCE. Feel free to leave anytime, Jon —

JON. Stop being a dick —

VINCE. — I won't get in your way this time —

JON. VINCENT!

End→ VINCE. *(Mimics.)* "VINCENT"! *(Suddenly Jon charges Vince and tackles him onto the bed. Entwined in each other's arms, they now wrestle ferociously, rolling together off the bed and onto the floor. The fight is not so much about the tape as about their anger with each other, which is intense, deep-rooted and filled with violent tendencies ... although there is also something oddly comic about this wrestling match, seeing as it is the exact type of "roughhousing" they might have done in sixth grade — and yet they are both twenty-eight. It continues, with both alternately gaining an upper edge ... until Jon gains an advantage on Vince by pinning him partially up against the base of the wall in a position that looks comfortable for neither man. They remain*

30

somewhat stuck here ... until there is a knock on the door. They stop struggling. Beats. Vincent disengages himself from Jon. Both boys are now in a state of semi-panic, with Jon looking for possible escape routes, and Vince straightening his hair and tidying the room ... After several hurried moments, Jon slips into the bathroom as Vince goes to the door and, still breathing quite heavily, opens it. Amy Randall, twenty-eight, enters. Vince's demeanor with Amy is like that of a somewhat stoned puppy-dog.) Hey, Amy —

AMY. Hi, Vincent. *(They give a brief, tentative but genuine hug.)*

VINCE. Wow. You look good.

AMY. You, too —

VINCE. Naw, it's nothing. *(Amy enters; Jon haltingly emerges from the bathroom as —)* You're not gonna believe who just showed up —

AMY. ... Jon?

JON. Hi, Amy.

AMY. Wow.

JON. Yeah.

AMY. ... Quite the reunion —

VINCE. He just swung by to say hello.

AMY. *(To Jon.)* I haven't seen you in ...

JON. Since high school, probably.

VINCE. I saw you at Tracy's, right?

AMY. That's right, about five years ago.

JON. I couldn't make it that time.

AMY. That's right. You were in grad school?

JON. USC.

AMY. For film? —

JON. Yeah.

AMY. Obviously — "Lansing Film Festival" —

JON. Right, that's why I'm here.

AMY. Right. Vince told me.

JON. Right —

AMY. Right. *(Beat ...)* I think I'm gonna wait outside, Vincent —

VINCE. No, don't.

AMY. It's just that I didn't lock my car.

VINCE. That's OK. Really. I can watch it from here. *(Vince looks out the window ...)* It's fine. *(Vince stands next to Amy, facing Jon.)* I'll just stand here.

31

AMY. O-K. *(Silence.)*
VINCE. So.
AMY. Yeah. *(Beat.)*
VINCE. It's good to see you, Amy.
AMY. You too, Vincent.
VINCE. *(Pause.)* So ... why do you live in Lansing?
AMY. I guess I like it. It's sort of mellow.
VINCE. Totally.
AMY. I went to school in Ann Arbor.
VINCE. That's right.
AMY. So I just decided to stay.
VINCE. I admire that.
JON. *(Beat.)* Vince told me but ... what kind of law is it — ?
AMY. I'm an assistant district attorney.
JON. Right. That's cool.
AMY. Yeah, I like it a lot.
JON. Yeah?
AMY. Definitely. It's good, it's a pretty good job.
JON. *(Pause.)* So you, like, what — you basically prosecute crim-inals?
AMY. Yeah.
JON. *(Pause.)* Cool.
AMY. Yeah. *(Beat.)* So what are *you* up to, Vincent?
VINCE. Me?
AMY. Yeah.
VINCE. Not much.
AMY. I can't believe you just called me out of the blue like that this morning.
VINCE. Yeah?
AMY. I actually love it when people do that.
VINCE. Why?
AMY. I don't know. I never have the courage to do that kind of thing.
VINCE. I just figured what the hell.
AMY. Yeah, but you could've easily *not* done it.
VINCE. Not what?
AMY. Not called. Most people don't.
JON. That's true.

AMY. It *is* true.

VINCE. Like Jon.

JON. *(In explanation.)* I didn't know you lived out here.

AMY. And if you had?

JON. I'm probably one of those people who don't have the courage.

AMY. You think?

JON. It's hard to say.

AMY. It is. Half the time it's not even worth it. People change, they end up having nothing to say to each other, even if they were best friends a year earlier.

VINCE. *(Beat.)* I'm glad you're not fat.

AMY. Is that right?

VINCE. Yeah.

AMY. You should of seen me in college.

VINCE. Fat?

AMY. Quite.

VINCE. Me too.

AMY. Probably for different reasons. *(Beat ...)* So, you didn't answer my question.

VINCE. Which one?

AMY. What are you doing these days?

VINCE. Oh. I live in California.

AMY. Where?

VINCE. Oakland.

AMY. ... Nice.

VINCE. I'm a firefighter.

AMY. Are you serious?

VINCE. I'm totally serious.

AMY. That's pretty cool, Vincent.

VINCE. It keeps me busy.

AMY. I'm sure.

VINCE. Yeah.

AMY. *(Beat.)* Lotta fires in Oakland?

VINCE. Average.

JON. I should get going.

VINCE. I thought you were coming to dinner with us.

JON. No, I never said that.

VINCE. Well why don't you?

JON. I can't, I gotta get some sleep for tomorrow.

VINCE. No you don't —

JON. Yeah, actually, I do —

VINCE. Dude, they're showing your *movie*, you're not running a marathon —

JON. I know, but —

VINCE. Plus they're showing it at two o'clock in the afternoon.

JON. I know, but I have some meetings in the morning.

AMY. You haven't changed, have you, Vincent?

VINCE. Whattayou mean?

AMY. I can remember you doing the exact same thing when we were dating.

VINCE. Doing what?

AMY. Putting pressure on people to follow whatever schedule you've already worked out in your head.

VINCE. That's not true.

AMY. It *is*, but it's nice. It's like you stayed up the night before thinking for hours how the next day was going to work and now you just want people to partake in your vision.

VINCE. OK, that's not true, Amy —

AMY. OK.

VINCE. Jon can do anything he wants —

AMY. I know —

VINCE. I'm just suggesting he joins us for dinner.

JON. Why?

VINCE. Because I'm sentimental. Is that so wrong? I like it when old friends get together. It makes me feel warm.

AMY. Maybe Jon doesn't feel like it —

VINCE. I know he doesn't because he doesn't have the courage. It's like you said, he lets these things go.

AMY. I didn't mean him specifically.

VINCE. Well you should have. He always does it.

JON. Does what?

VINCE. Lets things go. If you saw your mother on the street, you'd cross to the other side.

JON. What are you — high?

VINCE. Yes.

AMY. *(Pause.)* Are you high, Vincent?

34

VINCE. ... A bit.

AMY. You've been smoking pot since high school?

VINCE. It's no different than drinking —

AMY. I know, but do you also still drink? —

VINCE. So?

AMY. I'm just saying you should be careful —

VINCE. What is this, "Lecture Vince Night"?

AMY. Who's lecturing you?

VINCE. *You* are. *He* did, I'm waiting for the Motel 6 *desk* guy to come in here next.

AMY. It's only because I care about you.

VINCE. You haven't seen me for five years.

AMY. But you were my first boyfriend. It's inevitable. You could turn into a dirty old man and I'd still care.

VINCE. Really?

AMY. Of course. It's one of those things.

VINCE. *(Beat.)* Do you wanna get married?

AMY. I can't right now.

VINCE. Why?

AMY. I have a boyfriend.

VINCE. Who is he?

AMY. He's the district attorney.

VINCE. That is so typical! ...

AMY. Why?

VINCE. I don't know, it just is ...

AMY. If it doesn't work out, I'll give you a call in Oakland.

VINCE. Yeah, right —

JON. So I should get going.

VINCE. *(To Amy.)* Why don't you give *him* a lecture?

AMY. On what?

VINCE. Taking better care of himself.

AMY. He looks like he's doing OK.

JON. *(Standing.)* It was good to see you again, Amy.

VINCE. Whoa, whoa, whoa —

AMY. Vince —

VINCE. No, he's not getting out of here just like that.

JON. Maybe I'll see you tomorrow.

VINCE. No, bullshit! —

JON. Vince —

VINCE. What?!

JON. I have to go. *(Beat; Jon reaches out to shake Amy's hand.)*

VINCE. You see, it's actually really nice of you to say that, Amy, because I always thought *Jon* was your first love. *(Beat.)* I mean, I know you guys didn't really date that much, but I guess I always assumed — even though I didn't know about it 'til later — I always assumed that when you guys got together there at the end of senior year, it was sort of like some long-awaited love affair that was bound to happen. *(Beat.)* Am I characterizing that correctly?

JON. *(Beat.)* I don't think anyone would call it a long-awaited love affair, Vince.

VINCE. What would you call it?

JON. I'd call it us getting together at the end of senior year.

VINCE. *(Pause; to Amy.)* Oh. Maybe I'm just jealous because … you know, *I* wanted to be your first boyfriend.

AMY. You were.

VINCE. I know, but … you know what I mean.

AMY. Oh.

VINCE. I shouldn't care about that kind of stuff, but like I say, I'm sentimental.

AMY. That's not sentimental, Vincent.

VINCE. What is it?

AMY. It's stupid.

VINCE. … I agree, but see, I didn't know that in high school. Back then, you not wanting to have sex with me was sort of like being disinvited to Christmas dinner at my grandparents. *(Pause.)* Which is something I'm very sentimental about.

AMY. You shouldn't have taken it personally.

VINCE. I know, but I did. *(Pause.)* Especially when you guys ended up getting together. Literally. *(Quietly to Amy.)* But I guess I blew it out of proportion.

AMY. What're you talking about?

VINCE. I'm talking about you guys getting together at the end of senior year. It hurt my feelings at the time. But according to Jon, it was less of a long-awaited love affair and more like just two kids getting giddy before graduation. In which case, I suppose I really shouldn't hold a grudge. *(Beat.)* Is that what it was?

AMY. *(Beat.)* I would say that it was a crush that never amounted to much.

VINCE. For you or for him?

AMY. For me.

JON. Vince, it doesn't seem like Amy really wants to talk about this.

VINCE. Why not, we're all mature adults. We can talk about a high-school crush that happened ten years ago.

JON. Fine, then I'm gonna let you two have this discussion without me.

VINCE. OK, but before you leave, I'm just curious as to why nothing ever came of Amy's crush for you. Amy?

AMY. Why nothing ever came of it?

VINCE. Yeah. Why *didn't* it develop into something more serious. I mean, it wasn't like you and I got back together afterwards. I don't think you even dated anyone after that. At least not anybody from our school.

AMY. *(Beat.)* I guess it just didn't work out.

VINCE. Oh. *(Pause. Gentle:)* And there's no specific reason for that?

AMY. I'm sure there was.

VINCE. But?

AMY. No but. I'm sure there was.

VINCE. Oh. *(Beat.)* Why're you so anxious to leave, Jon?

JON. Because this is awkward for me.

VINCE. And so you'd rather *leave?*

JON. Fine, Vince. *(He stretches his arms out, palms up.)* Here I am. Would anyone like to say anything to me? *(Silence.)* Amy?

AMY. *(Beat ...)* No thanks.

JON. Vince?

VINCE. Yeah. *(Vince takes the tape from his pocket and tosses it to Jon.)* It's your call, Jon. I can't speak for you. *(Jon holds the tape; silence.)*

JON. *(Beat ...)* It was good to see you again, Amy.

AMY. *(Pause.)* You too.

VINCE. *(To self.)* That is so fucking typical ...

JON. I gotta go. *(Jon prepares to leave, with a small, unsuccessful attempt to make eye contact with Amy before doing so ... He opens the door —)*

VINCE. Jon?

JON. What?

VINCE. Can I have that back? *(Beat ... Jon tosses Vince the tape; beat.)*

JON. Goodbye, Amy. *(She does not answer. Beat; Jon exits. Silence ...)*

AMY. Oakland must be a pretty safe place.

VINCE. Why?

AMY. There don't seem to be enough fires to keep you busy.

VINCE. What do you mean?

AMY. Can you tell me what that was about?

VINCE. I wanted to know what happened between you two.

AMY. When?

VINCE. That night. *(Beat.)* I wanted him to apologize to you.

AMY. Why?

VINCE. So you could hear it. *(Beat.)* He admitted it to me.

AMY. What did you do?

VINCE. I got him to admit it. It's on the tape.

AMY. Admit what?

VINCE. What he did to you. *(No answer.)* He did do it, didn't he? Amy? *(Beat.)* That night. Am I wrong? *(Beat. Gentle:)* He raped you. Didn't he?

AMY. *(Pause.)* Why would that be any of your business?

VINCE. You're missing my point —

AMY. And even if he had, the last thing I would want is a taped confession.

VINCE. Why not?

AMY. Because I'm not the one who needs it.

VINCE. What're you talking about? *(She starts to leave.)*

AMY. I'm not the one who needs it.

VINCE. So then who needs it?

AMY. I'll see you later —

VINCE. Where are you going?

AMY. Home.

VINCE. I don't think you understand, I was trying to do the right thing.

AMY. *(Turning back to him.)* For whom?

VINCE. For you.

AMY. Is that really what you mean, Vincent?

38

VINCE. Of course it's what I mean! —

AMY. Because I don't think it is.

VINCE. I thought you'd appreciate it.

AMY. Well I don't.

VINCE. Why not?

AMY. Because he didn't rape me. *(Beats.)*

VINCE. What? *(Pause.)*

AMY. He didn't. *(Pause.)* So the only person you're trying to make feel better is yourself. *(Silence. Beat. Then a knock on the door. Beat. Vince puts the tape back in his pocket. He goes and opens the door. Jon is there. He looks at them both; beat.)*

JON. Hey.

VINCE. *(Pause.)* Hey. *(Jon closes the door behind him and enters the room more fully; more silence.)* What are you doing?

JON. I came back.

VINCE. Why?

JON. Because I felt like it. *(Beat.)* Vince, can you give us a couple minutes in private?

VINCE. *(Beat.)* Are you kidding me?

JON. I'm serious.

VINCE. You want me to leave you alone with her?

JON. Yeah —

VINCE. No —

JON. You can wait outside the door.

VINCE. No fucking way!

JON. Why not?

VINCE. Because of the whole — no. No.

JON. I just need two minutes —

VINCE. Why?

JON. I want to tell her something.

VINCE. What?

JON. It's none of your business.

VINCE. Yes it is —

JON. Why?

VINCE. Because I'm the one who brought it up!

AMY. It's all right, Vincent.

VINCE. No it's not.

AMY. Yes it is.

39

VINCE. Well I don't care, I'm not leaving! *(Vince folds his arms and sits down. Silence. Beat; Jon approaches Amy …)*
JON. I wanted to apologize.
VINCE. For what?
JON. Vince —
VINCE. What?!
JON. Shut up! *(Beat; to Amy, genuine.)* I wanted to apologize. *(Beat.)* For what it's worth. *(Pause.)* I'm sorry. I really, honestly, truly am. *(Silence …)*
AMY. For what?
JON. For what happened between us in high school.
AMY. What happened between us?
JON. I'm talking about what happened at the end of senior year, which Vince was trying to get me to talk about before.
AMY. Before when?
JON. Like five minutes ago.
AMY. About when you and I got together in high school?
JON. Right.
AMY. Right. So tell me again what happened?
JON. *(Beat.)* Do you know which day I'm talking about?
AMY. At the end of senior year? At Rebecca's party?
JON. Yeah.
AMY. Yeah.
VINCE. *(Beat.)* What are you guys doing?
AMY. I'm just curious. I don't want there to be a communication gap here.
JON. I'm not sure what I'm supposed to say.
AMY. I think you think you did something to me.
JON. Yes.
AMY. What do you think you did?
JON. Why?
AMY. Because this is very interesting to me.
JON. Do you not think something happened?
AMY. Well of course something happened.
JON. But are you saying you don't remember what it was?
AMY. C'mon, Jon — there are certain things one doesn't forget.
JON. I agree.
AMY. I'm just wondering how you would describe it.

40

JON. Probably the same way as you.

AMY. You think?

JON. *(Beat.)* The whole reason this thing started is because Vince taped this conversation he and I had earlier.

VINCE. Dude, I'm sorry —

JON. It's fine —

VINCE. I didn't realize —

JON. I'm just saying, that that's why I'm here.

AMY. You're here because Vince taped you?

JON. Yes.

AMY. Why?

JON. *Why?*

AMY. Why?

JON. … Because it made me think.

AMY. Oh.

JON. Which is why I came back.

AMY. Good — so tell me what happened.

JON. *(Beat …)* I think I raped you.

AMY. *(Beat …)* No. You didn't rape me.

JON. *(Beat.)* Yes I did.

AMY. No. You didn't.

JON. *(Beat.)* Are you trying to make fun of this?

AMY. No.

JON. Amy. I *know* what happened.

AMY. Apparently not.

JON. I do.

AMY. Says who?

JON. Me.

AMY. Why?

JON. Because I just admitted it.

AMY. On what — the tape?

JON. Yeah.

AMY. What's on it?

JON. It's me confessing what I did.

AMY. What did you do?

JON. I just told you.

AMY. But that doesn't prove you *did* it —

JON. Why not? —

41

AMY. Because if no one's accusing you of anything, then there's no reason to confess.

JON. ... I'm having trouble realizing what you're doing.

AMY. I'm not doing anything —

JON. This is not an easy thing for me.

AMY. You sure about that?

VINCE. Jon?

JON. What?

VINCE. Do you know what you're saying?

JON. I'm saying what you wanted me to say.

VINCE. But are you sure you have the right girl?

JON. Yes!

VINCE. She says nothing happened.

JON. She's lying —

AMY. No I'm not.

JON. Amy?!

AMY. What?

JON. You're mocking this!

AMY. Why would I do that?

JON. I don't know, but if you are, I have better things to do.

AMY. I just think we just have differing perceptions of what happened.

JON. I really don't see how that could be.

AMY. Why, because *you* decided you did something?

JON. I *did* do something.

AMY. Well I say you didn't.

JON. So then what happened?

AMY. We had sex.

JON. Amy, I'm trying to be honest.

AMY. Why now?

JON. Because I haven't *seen* you in ten years.

AMY. But why *now?*

JON. Because when Vince played me back that tape, it hit me what I had done.

AMY. And if he *hadn't* played back the tape?

JON. Yeah — ?

AMY. Would you be saying this?

JON. Probably not.

42

AMY. Or is it just that I'm here?

JON. What do you mean?

AMY. If I lived in Alaska, would you have sought me out?

JON. I don't really know.

AMY. You should look into that.

JON. Fine.

AMY. Or is it that you're jealous.

JON. Of what?

AMY. Vincent and I.

JON. That's ridiculous —

AMY. Why? *I* loved *you*. *(Beat.)* I did. I was totally in love with you that night. *(Beat ...)* Did you love me?

JON. *(Beat.)* No.

AMY. So why were you with me?

JON. I'm not sure.

AMY. Maybe it's the same reason you came back to apologize just now.

JON. Which is what?

AMY. You like pissing off Vincent.

JON. Why would it piss him off if that's what he wanted in the first place!?

AMY. Because he's confused.

VINCE. Exactly.

AMY. It's never too late to one-up your best friend by telling him once and for all that you raped the love of his life in high school. *(Pause.)* Especially if you get to do it in front of her.

JON. You really think I'm like that?

AMY. I don't know, I have a very poor record of judging you accurately. *(Beat.)* Maybe you just came back to get the last word. You didn't like what was on the tape, so you came back to hear yourself phrase it more eloquently.

JON. *(Beat.)* The reason I came back is to apologize, which I can assure you is not at all disingenuous. I honestly am sorry.

AMY. Why, because you had your hand over my mouth?

JON. *(Pause.)* Yes.

AMY. Well hey, Jon ... I let everybody do that. *(Beat.)*

JON. Can you please just tell me the truth?

AMY. I am. *(Beats ... Jon starts for the door.)*

43

VINCE. Where are you going?

JON. I think I should leave.

VINCE. Why? —

JON. Because no matter what I say, there's nowhere for this to go.

AMY. *(Strong.)* You want the last word, Jon, but it's not yours to have.

VINCE. Why don't you guys just figure out what the fuck you're talking about?! —

JON. Vince!

VINCE. What?

JON. She's in denial.

VINCE. Amy?

AMY. *(To Vince.)* What was it that even made you think something happened?

VINCE. At Rebecca's?

AMY. Yeah.

VINCE. Because I thought it did. I thought later that that's what you were trying to tell me.

AMY. Why?

VINCE. Because why else would you have slept with Jon when you were supposed to be dating me?

AMY. You and I had already broken up.

VINCE. I know, but we hadn't even slept together, so what the hell were you doing sleeping with him?

AMY. It's none of your business.

VINCE. Well that's partly why I figured something happened.

AMY. Why, because if I wasn't sleeping with you, why would I sleep with somebody else?

VINCE. Yeah ... I guess ... I guess ... I thought something like that. *(Beat ...)*

JON. I'm gonna go. *(To Vince.)* Maybe I'll see you tomorrow. Amy, I'm sorry. And I'm sorry you're not in a place where you can hear that right now. *(Pause.)* I hope you have a good life. *(Jon heads for the door.)*

AMY. Why did you say that?

JON. What?

AMY. That I'm not in a place to hear that.

JON. Because you don't seem to realize that I'm serious. I don't know how else to put it to you other than to say what I've said. Even if you really do think it wasn't a big deal, it was for me, and I want you to know that I'm sorry it happened. *(Jon finishes, his words lingering in the air a moment. He has made Amy think. It seems as though she will not answer him.)*

AMY. *(Beat; calm on the surface.)* Well you *should* be. And I hope you die for it and go to hell; and if there is no hell, I hope that you suffer on your way *to* death, and that your last living sensation is that of a steel rod being shoved repeatedly up your insides so that it batters your heart and punctures your stomach; and when you die and your sphincter finally collapses, my hope is that your last bowel movement be saturated with blood from the draining backwash of your rotted, fucking, pathetic guts! *(Long silence as she "recovers." To Vince, calm.)* Is that along the lines of what you wanted? *(No answer; beat ... to Jon.)* I really don't know what you want me to say to you.

JON. *(Pause.)* Nothing. *(Beat. Amy has pulled a cell phone from her purse and now calmly dials three numbers ...)*

AMY. *(Into her phone.)* Yes, this is Amy Randall from the D.A.'s office, could you please dispatch a squad car over to the Motel 6 on Saginaw, room thirty-two. There seems to be a significant amount of illegal substance in the room ... it appears to be cocaine ... yes, and also, you might want to run a check on one of the two gentlemen here, Jon Saltzman S-a-l-t-z-m-a-n — possible history of sexual misconduct including a verified first degree CSC ten years prior ... thank you. *(Amy folds the phone and returns it to her purse. Silence. Jon and Vince are both staring at her. Beat.)* You guys can make a run for it if you like.

VINCE. Did you really just do that?

AMY. The average response time in Lansing is four minutes. It's one of the top departments in the country.

JON. Why does it have to be like this?

AMY. Because if you're truly repentant, then you should be willing to pay the price.

JON. Why can't you just accept the fact that I'm sorry?

AMY. It does me no good.

JON. Is that *my* fault?

AMY. No, that's the way it is.

JON. But *I'm* the one who has to run out of here like a criminal?
AMY. It's up to you.
JON. Because I'm not going to.
AMY. Is that because you think the statute of limitations ran out?
JON. I have no idea.
AMY. There is none for a sexual misconduct felony. *(Pause.)* Just to let you know.
VINCE. *(Beat.)* Okay — I really don't feel like getting busted for a couple lines of coke.
AMY. Then I guess I'll see you later, Vincent. *(Vincent is unsure what to do for a moment, then he quickly wipes the rest of the cocaine back into the bag and sticks it in his pocket.)* Just do me a favor and leave that tape behind. *(Pause.)* So I can give it to Officer Friendly. *(Pause; Vince is quite unsure what to do.)*
VINCE. You want me to give you the tape?
AMY. Yeah. *(Vince looks at Jon.)* You don't need his permission.
VINCE. I feel like I do.
AMY. You didn't need his permission to *make* it; why would you need it now?
VINCE. *(Pause.)* Protocol?
AMY. Fine, then I'll just stay here and tell them myself. *(Vince starts to gather up his things.)*
VINCE. Dude, it might be in your best interest to come with me.
JON. I'm staying.
VINCE. Why?!
JON. Because maybe she's right: Maybe I should pay the price.
VINCE. Fine but what about me?!
JON. What about you?
VINCE. *I* didn't really do anything wrong!
AMY. You're in possession of illegal substance —
VINCE. I know but I was just trying to blow off some steam.
AMY. You should've blown it off with beer.
VINCE. I *did,* I just needed to blow off a little extra.
JON. You better go, Vince, they're on their way.
VINCE. Come with me.
JON. No.
VINCE. Don't be an idiot, they'll arrest you!! *(Jon remains still. To Amy.)* Is this really what you want?

46

AMY. Jon's a big boy, he can make his own decisions.

VINCE. Fine, then I'm outta here.

JON. Thanks, Vince.

VINCE. What?

JON. Thanks —

VINCE. For what?

JON. For all your honesty.

VINCE. *(At a loss.)* What do you mean?

JON. Nothing. I'll see you later. *(Vince starts again for the door, but then stops. He knows he wouldn't be able to live with himself if he left — for it is he who got Jon into this.)*

VINCE. FUCK! *(In a change of plans, he now hurriedly takes the bag of coke from his pocket, then reaches into his duffel bag and produces an enormous bag of marijuana; he then takes both bags and goes into the bathroom. We hear the flush of a toilet. A moment later, Vincent comes back out empty-handed; he goes to the table and attempts to wipe clean any potential remnants of the cocaine. All of this is done with a large amount of frustration and bitter dejection. He then goes to the window and looks out. Seeing that he still has at least a minute or two, he takes the cassette from his pocket, looks momentarily at Jon, then methodically breaks the cassette in half, pulling out the tape so as to ensure the cassette's total destruction. Finally, he sits on the bed. Silence. There is silence for quite awhile as the three of them sit, some perhaps looking at others. Then, a notion slowly begins to enter Vince's mind. Beat ...)* [OPTION: Vince does NOT break the tape before Amy leaves, but rather Vince takes it out after Amy exits and it is included as part of the final blackout image of Jon and Vince at the end of the play.] Did you really call the police?

AMY. No.

VINCE. *Jesus Christ!!!*

AMY. Sorry.

VINCE. *Why'd you do that?!!*

AMY. I felt like it.

VINCE. YOU ARE SO *FUCKED* UP!!!

AMY. What did you expect?

VINCE. *(Beat ... a broken man.)* ... Fine, but do you know how much those drugs cost?

AMY. There'll be other drugs, Vincent.

47

VINCE. I know, but I really liked *those* ones. *(Silence … Amy now stands; she regards Jon for a very long moment.)*

AMY. *(Beat, to Jon.)* Good luck tomorrow.

JON. Thank you.

AMY. Goodbye, Vincent.

VINCE. Bye, Amy. *(Amy opens the door to go.)* It was good to see — *(Amy exits, closing the door behind her. Beats. Jon and Vince sit in silence. Vince starts to say something, then decides not to. Beats … Lights fade to black.)*

End of Play

AUTHOR'S NOTE

Tape may be performed in one of two ways:

First option is to perform just the single-set one-act play —
beginning with the stage directions in which Vince is pouring and
drinking beers and ending with Vince and Jon alone in the motel
room, unable to say anything to one another.

Second option is to include the following prologue and epilogue.
In this case, one would, obviously, begin with the prologue, then
jump from the offstage voices/video prologue directly into Vince
opening the door to Jon as the dialogue begins (thus excising the
beer-pouring/drinking stage directions). Then, at the play's finish,
we would cross fade into the epilogue's three monologues.

It is the author's wish that the play be performed with either prologue and entire epilogue or with just the motel-room section.
(And yet there is, of course, a third option, which is to perform the
prologue and the Amy monologue of the epilogue, thus cutting
out the Vince and Jon parts of the epilogue.)

OPTIONAL PROLOGUE

A darkened room, lit mainly by the glow of a television set. The voices of two young men can be heard from beyond an open doorway, through which smoke intermittently emanates. Party music can be heard from the other room. (Or: The entire prologue could be seen on a large video projected onto the back wall.)

VINCE. Why — for fuck's sake?!!
JON. Maybe she just needed to move on.
VINCE. But we were in love!
JON. Wait — save it for the video.
VINCE. Is it working?
JON. Almost.
VINCE. Did you put the thing in the thing?
JON. What?
VINCE. Put the red thing in the red thing!
JON. That's what she said last night.
VINCE. Dude, that is so fucking stupid. It's like a third-grader.
JON. That's what she said last night.
VINCE. I'm switching to the bong.
JON. Vince?
VINCE. What?
JON. If I'm a banker, in like twenty years — ?
VINCE. Yeah?
JON. I want you to come and find me, and kill me.
VINCE. You don't like bankers?
JON. It's what everybody expects.
VINCE. I expect you to be a dickwad in twenty years.
JON. Well if I'm a dickwad, then it probably means I'm also a banker.
VINCE. Why — all bankers are dickwads?

JON. You're not listening —

VINCE. I'm totally listening and frankly I find it offensive to bankers!

JON. Whatever. *(Sound of a bong.)*

VINCE. Why do you fucking *have* a camcorder anyway?

JON. Because I'm chronicling things.

VINCE. Chronicling what?

JON. Things!! We're graduating in two weeks — this is the last time we are who we are.

VINCE. Dude — smoke this.

JON. Hang on —

VINCE. *SMOKE IT!!*

JON. I think it's working. *(The light from the TV reflects moving images.)*

VINCE. Hey, I look like Ralph Macchio!

JON. *(Narrates.)* OK — senior year in high school: Whattayou got to say, Vince?

VINCE. If I'm a banker in twenty years, I want you to find me and give me a mammoth frickin' bong hit!!!!

JON. *(Still narrating.)* There you have it: folks: The goals and dreams of our next generation.

VINCE. Fuck —

JON. What?

VINCE. Amy's here.

JON. Vince — you gotta get over it.

VINCE. But she looks hot.

JON. She *is* hot.

VINCE. So — ?

JON. So that's it. Two weeks from now, it's a whole new fucking ball game!!

OPTIONAL EPILOGUE

*Lights rise on Vince, now dressed in casual Eddie Bauer wear,
sound of a phone ringing, followed by a machine picking up.*

JON. *(Voice-over.)* It's Jon, you know what to do. *(Sound of a beep.)*
VINCE. Hey, John. Vince here. *(Pause.)* How are you, man? It's been a long time. *(Pause.)* I actually tried calling you a few weeks ago, but ... your machine said you were on location ... in Antarctica, or somewhere, so ... I didn't leave a message.

Anyway, I've been thinking about you, I guess. *(Beat.)* You'll be happy to know that I finally woke up, after far too many years of not really waking up at all, waking and baking, waking and faking ... flaking. I quit the bullshit in Oakland, moved home for awhile, and then about a year ago, I moved up here. To Lansing. *(Beat.)* Which probably strikes you as funny, considering everything, but you know what? — it makes sense. *(Pause.)* There's some really fine dining out here. *(A small smile; beat.)* Anyway, I'm working as a high-school math teacher. I'm also assistant J.V. head football coach. We got robbed last week, fucking Upper Peninsula refs ... Anyway, I'm living a pretty quiet life. It's good.

(Beat; deep breath.) I guess the reason I wanted to check in is because about a month ago ... I gave Amy a call. *(Beat.)* We met at a T.G.I. Friday's. I ordered a Diet Coke, she had a glass of merlot. And we talked. *(Pause.)* And I apologized. For what happened five years ago ... in the motel room. *(Pause.)* And she didn't accept. Which was good. And which I'd expected. *(Beat.)*

I've been in love with her for seventeen years, Jon. I have. And just because it started in high school, does that make it wrong? If a person strips away everything about them that's stupid ... down to where only the fundamental feelings are left ... and those feelings are the same as they were when they first met, then aren't they legitimate? *(Pause.)* And I know that change is … it's a long-term thing … but my question to myself — and maybe to you — is: If enough of it has occurred in a person, can't they try again? *(Beat.)* I don't think about her every day. I date other women, I like my job. *(Pause.)* But I have hope. *(Pause.)* And maybe one of these days I'll try again. *(Beat.)*

I'm not sure why I'm telling you all this. You're probably busy, I just … I guess I just wanted to … let you know. *(Pause.)* I hope Antarctica treated you well and that you didn't … lose your penis to frostbite. *(Pause.)* Let's talk soon. Love you. *(Beat …)*

OPERATOR. *(Voice-over.)* If you'd like to make a call, please hang up and try your call again; if you'd like to make a call, please hang up and try your call again. *(Loud noise which accompanies that message … as lights cross-fade to Jon, who sits in a large armchair speaking to us tight-shot on camera, through a projected, highly defined digital video image.)*

JON. Archive, April third. *(Beat.)* This is gonna sound completely off the wall but I'm just gonna say it: I've been thinking about becoming a Unitarian minister. That's what I've been thinking about. *(Beat.)*

Unitarianism is an incredibly profound religion, to a great extent, I believe, because of its use of intuition. And keep in mind that we're in a day and age when no one really intuits anymore. We do just about everything *but* intuit. We insist, demand, deduce, ascertain, "base on faith," kill. Everything but intuit. Except for the Unitarians. These people intuit everything, not the least of which is God. They find God manifested in a grain of sand; in the glint of a lizard's eye. And I have to say that appeals to me. Because frankly I'm tired. I'm tired of … using plastic silverware and talking about yoga. *(Pause.)* I really just wanna live a more honest life.

(Beat.) I found these tapes the other day. Mostly stupid shit, me interviewing friends, blabbering about the end of high school. *(Pause.)* And I thought of Vince. *(Beat.)* I literally haven't seen the guy in ten years. Since that night in the motel room. We've talked, e-mailed, done all the peripheral shit. But we haven't seen each other. *(Beat.)* So I called him. Up there in Michigan. And I said, "Hey Vince, what're you doing?" And he said, "I'm raising my kid." And I said, "How is it?" And he said, "It's great, Jon, it really, truly is."

And when I hung up, I thought about the last time I saw him. And I thought, "Jesus Christ we've changed. Vince has a kid, he's not a drunk, he's ... happy." And then, inevitably — maybe because I'm a filmmaker, or because I'm a shitty Hollywood film-maker — I inevitably looked in the mirror, and I asked myself if *I'd* changed. Over ten years. Over twenty. *(Pause.)* And to tell you the truth, I wasn't sure what the answer was. *(Jon now points a remote control device in the direction of the camera and zooms very close-up on his still-youthful face; pause; very honest.)*

I've thought about nothing over the last ten years except for what happened that night. Nothing. I've made six movies, I've bought a house with a fucking swing that swings out over the Pacific, and I've been married and divorced and occasionally in love, but I have thought about nothing except that night. *(Beat.)* And maybe that sounds like bullshit, unless you know the kinds of thought I'm talking about, the late-night kinds when you're driv-ing near cliffs, when you're banging a twenty-two-year-old, when you're staring at the wall with a bottle of Aleve in your fucking hand. *(Beat.)* And if you asked me what I've thought about exactly, all those years — I wouldn't have a clue what to answer. It's not guilt, it's not my lost friendship with Vince, it's not even Amy so much, if truth be told. *(Pause.)* I've just thought. *(Beat.)* About who I am. Who I'm not. Who I would like to be capable of being. *(Beat.)* And the thing, or perhaps I should say, the only thing that I've come up with after ten years ... is that I think I wanna be a Unitarian minister. *(Beat.)*

I'm thirty-eight years old. *(Pause.)* I have a lot of time left. *(Jon now points a remote control device in the direction of the camera ... and turns himself off. He then presses another button and ... a moment later, Amy's grainy image appears on a dated, handheld cam-corder; she's dressed a bit like an early Madonna.)*
JON. *(Voice-over.)* Archive, Rebecca's party, May eighteenth —
AMY. What are you doing?
JON. *(Voice-over.)* It's like a chronicle ... about ... whatever, the end of school. Like ... like what do you think everything's gonna be like after graduation?
AMY. I dunno. I mean, I'll definitely miss things.
JON. *(Voice-over.)* Like Vince?

AMY. No. *(Pause.)* I mean, yeah, but ... *you* saw him just now —
he gets pissed, slams the door and now he'll drive around drunk all
night listening to like, *Yaz,* or whatever. *(Pause.)* You're not gonna
show him this, are you?
JON. *(Voice-over.)* No.
AMY. I dunno ... I keep having this dream where after graduation I take everything I've done for the last four years and put it
in, like, a crystal box ... and blow the whole thing to fucking
smithereens. And just walk away forever. *(Beat.)*

But then sometimes in the dream I *keep* the box — instead of
blowing it away — so that whenever I'm lost or fucked up, I can
retrace my steps back and crawl inside and say, "Yeah, this is where
I came from. This is who I am."

I dunno. I guess *neither* of those are ... *realistic.* 'Cause you
can't really *destroy* your past, and you also can't crawl back inside
it. *(Pause.)* Maybe the best we can do is sort of ... drag the box
along behind us ... and occasionally look inside ... and appreciate
its beauty. *(Beat; Amy looks at the camera, then smiles embarrassingly
... and perhaps flirtatiously ...)* What? ... *What?*

End of Play

PROPERTY LIST

Schlitz beer cans (VINCE)
Duffel bag (VINCE)
Joint (VINCE)
Lighter or matches (VINCE)
Phone (VINCE)
Tape recorder and tape (VINCE)
Sticker label (VINCE)
Pen or pencil (VINCE)
Plastic bag of cocaine (VINCE)
Credit card (VINCE)
Purse (AMY)
Cell phone (AMY)
Bag of marijuana (VINCE)
Remote control (JON)

SOUND EFFECTS

Music
Person inhaling through a bong
Taped dialogue
Phone ringing
Toilet flushing
Voice-over of answering machine
Phone operator voice-over followed by loud noise